Poems of Nature (annota

by Henry David Thoreau

INTRODUCTION

The fifty poems here brought together under the title 'Poems of Nature' are perhaps two-thirds of those which Thoreau preserved. Many of them were printed by him, in whole or in part, among his early contributions to Emerson's Dial, or in his own two volumes, The Week and Walden, which were all that were issued in his lifetime. Others were given to Mr. Sanborn for publication, by Sophia Thoreau, the year after her brother's death (several appeared in the Boston Commonwealth in 1863); or have been furnished from time to time by Mr. Blake, his literary executor.

Most of Thoreau's poems were composed early in his life, before his twenty-sixth year. 'Just now,' he wrote in the autumn of 1841, 'I am in the mid-sea of verses, and they actually rustle round me, as the leaves would round the head of Autumnus himself, should he thrust it up through some vales which I know; but, alas! many of them are but crisped and yellow leaves like his, I fear, and will deserve no better fate than to make mould for new harvests.' After 1843 he seems to have written but few poems, and had destroyed perhaps as many as he had retained, because they did not meet the exacting requirements of his friend Emerson, upon whose opinion at that time he placed great reliance. This loss was regretted by Thoreau in after years, when the poetical habit had left him, for he fancied that some of the verses were better than his friend had supposed. But Emerson, who seldom changed his mind, adhered to his verdict, and while praising some of the poems highly, perhaps extravagantly, would admit but a small number of them to the slight selection which he appended to the posthumous edition of Thoreau's Letters, edited by him in 1865; and even these were printed, in some instances, in an abbreviated and imperfect form.[1] A few other poems, with some translations from the Greek, have lately been included by Thoreau's Boston publishers in their volume of Miscellanies (vol. x. of the Riverside Edition, 1894). But no collection so full as the present one has ever been offered to the public.

It has not been attempted to make this a complete collection of Thoreau's poems, because, as has been well said, 'many of them seem to be merely pendants to his prose discourse, dropped in as forcible epigrams where they are brief, and in other instances made ancillary to the idea just expressed, or to perpetuate a distinct conception that has some vital connection with the point from which it was poured forth. It is, therefore, almost an injustice to treat them separately at all.'[2] After the discontinuance of The Dial, Thoreau ceased to publish his verses as separate poems, but interpolated them, in the manner described, in his prose essays, where they form a sort of accompaniment to the thought, and from which it is in many cases impossible to detach them. That he himself set some value on them in this connection may be gathered from a sentence in the last of his published letters, in which he writes to a correspondent: 'I am pleased when you say that in The Week you like especially those little snatches of poetry interspersed through the book, for these I suppose are the least attractive to most readers?'

Everything that concerns a great writer has its special interest; and Thoreau's poetry, whatever its intrinsic value may be, is full of personal significance; in fact, as Emerson remarked, 'his biography is in his verses.' Thus, many of these poems will be found to throw light on certain passages of his life. 'Inspiration,' for example, is the record of his soul's awakening to the new impulse of transcendentalism; the stanzas on 'Sympathy' perhaps contain in a thinly disguised form the story of his youthful love, and the sacrifice which he imposed on himself to avoid rivalry with his brother; the lines 'To my Brother' refer to the sudden and tragic death of John Thoreau in 1842; and 'The Departure' is believed to be the poem in which Henry Thoreau, when leaving in 1843 the home of Emerson, where he had lived for two years, took farewell of his friends. The numerous other allusions to the life and scenery of Concord, with which Thoreau's own life was so closely blended, require no comment or explanation.

Thoreau's view of the poetic character, as stated by him in The Week, is illustrative of his own position. 'A true poem,' he says, 'is distinguished not so much by a felicitous expression, or any thought it suggests, as by the atmosphere which surrounds it. There are two classes of men called poets. The one cultivates life, the other art: one seeks food for nutriment, the other for flavor; one satisfies hunger, the other gratifies the palate.' There can be no doubt to which of these classes Thoreau himself belongs. If metrical skill be insisted on as an indispensable condition of poetry, he can hardly be ranked among the poets; nor, where this criterion was dominant, was it surprising that, as one of his contemporaries tells us,[3] with reference to his verses in The Dial, 'an unquenchable laughter, like that of the gods at Vulcan's limping, went up over his ragged and halting lines.' But in the appreciation of poetry there is a good deal more to be considered than this; and, as the same writer has remarked, there is 'a frank and unpretending nobleness' in many of Thoreau's verses, distinguished as they are, at their best, by their ripe fulness of thought, quiet gravity of tone, and epigrammatic terseness of expression. The title of poet could hardly be withheld from the author of such truly powerful pieces as 'The Fall of the Leaf,' 'Winter Memories,' 'Smoke in Winter,' or 'Inspiration.'

Nor should it be forgotten that Thoreau was always regarded as a poet by those who were associated with him. 'Poet-Naturalist' was the suggestive title which Ellery Channing applied to him; and Hawthorne remarked that 'his thoughts seem to measure and attune themselves into spontaneous verse, as they rightfully may, since there is real poetry in them.' Even Emerson's final estimate was far from unappreciative. 'His poetry,' he wrote in his biographical sketch, 'might be bad or good; he no doubt wanted a lyric facility and technical skill, but he had the source of poetry in his spiritual perception. His own verses are often rude and defective. The gold does not yet run pure—is drossy and crude. The thyme and marjoram are not yet honey. But if he want lyric fineness and technical merits, if he have not the poetic temperament, he never lacks the causal thought, showing that his genius was better than his talent.'

Perhaps what Thoreau said of Quarles, one of that school of gnomic poets of which he was a student, might be aptly applied to himself: 'It is rare to find one who was so much of a poet and so little of an artist. Hopelessly quaint, he never doubts his genius; it is only he and his God in all the world. He uses language sometimes as greatly as Shakespeare; and though there is not much straight grain in him, there is plenty of rough, crooked timber.' The affinity of Thoreau's style to that of Herbert, Donne, Cowley, and other minor Elizabethans, has often been remarked; and it has been truly said that the stanzas 'Sic Vita' might almost have a niche in Herbert's Temple.

It must be granted, then, that Thoreau, whatever his limitations, had the poet's vision, and sometimes the poet's divine faculty; and if this was manifested more frequently in his masterly prose, it was neither absent from his verse nor from the whole tenor of his character. It was his destiny to be one of the greatest prose writers whom America has produced, and he had a strong, perhaps an exaggerated, sense of the dignity of this calling. 'Great prose,' he thinks, 'of equal elevation, commands our respect more than great verse, since it implies a more permanent and level height, a life more pervaded with the grandeur of the thought. The poet only makes an irruption, like a Parthian, and is off again, shooting while he retreats; but the prose writer has conquered, like a Roman, and settled colonies.'

If therefore, we cannot unreservedly place Thoreau among the poetical brotherhood, we may at least recognise that he was a poet in the larger sense in which his friends so regarded, him—he felt, thought, acted, and lived as a poet, though he did not always write as one. In his own words—

'My life has been the poem I would have writ,
But I could not both live and utter it.'
Such qualities dignify life and make the expression of it memorable, not perhaps immediately, to the multitude of readers, but at first to an appreciative few, and eventually to a wide circle of mankind.

NATURE

O Nature! I do not aspire
To be the highest in thy quire,—
To be a meteor in the sky,
Or comet that may range on high;
Only a zephyr that may blow
Among the reeds by the river low;
Give me thy most privy place
Where to run my airy race.

In some withdrawn, unpublic mead
Let me sigh upon a reed,
Or in the woods, with leafy din,
Whisper the still evening in:
Some still work give me to do,—
Only—be it near to you!

INSPIRATION

Whate'er we leave to God, God does,
And blesses us;
The work we choose should be our own,
God leaves alone.

If with light head erect I sing,
Though all the Muses lend their force,
From my poor love of anything,
The verse is weak and shallow as its source.

But if with bended neck I grope
Listening behind me for my wit,
With faith superior to hope,
More anxious to keep back than forward it;

Making my soul accomplice there
Unto the flame my heart hath lit,
Then will the verse for ever wear—
Time cannot bend the line which God hath writ.

Always the general show of things
Floats in review before my mind,
And such true love and reverence brings,
That sometimes I forget that I am blind.

But now there comes unsought, unseen,
Some clear divine electuary,
And I, who had but sensual been,
Grow sensible, and as God is, am wary.

I hearing get, who had but ears,
And sight, who had but eyes before,
I moments live, who lived but years,
And truth discern, who knew but learning's lore.

I hear beyond the range of sound,
I see beyond the range of sight,
New earths and skies and seas around,
And in my day the sun doth pale his light.

A clear and ancient harmony
Pierces my soul through all its din,
As through its utmost melody,—
Farther behind than they, farther within.

More swift its bolt than lightning is,
Its voice than thunder is more loud,
It doth expand my privacies

To all, and leave me single in the crowd.

It speaks with such authority,
With so serene and lofty tone,
That idle Time runs gadding by,
And leaves me with Eternity alone.

Now chiefly is my natal hour,
And only now my prime of life,
Of manhood's strength it is the flower,
'Tis peace's end and war's beginning strife.

It comes in summer's broadest noon,
By a grey wall or some chance place,
Unseasoning Time, insulting June,
And vexing day with its presuming face.

Such fragrance round my couch it makes,
More rich than are Arabian drugs,
That my soul scents its life and wakes
The body up beneath its perfumed rugs.

Such is the Muse, the heavenly maid,
The star that guides our mortal course,
Which shows where life's true kernel 's laid,
Its wheat's fine flour, and its undying force.

She with one breath attunes the spheres,
And also my poor human heart,
With one impulse propels the years
Around, and gives my throbbing pulse its start.

I will not doubt for evermore,
Nor falter from a steadfast faith,

For though the system be turned o'er,
God takes not back the word which once he saith.

I will not doubt the love untold
Which not my worth nor want has bought,
Which wooed me young, and wooes me old,
And to this evening hath me brought.

My memory I'll educate
To know the one historic truth,
Remembering to the latest date
The only true and sole immortal youth.

Be but thy inspiration given,
No matter through what danger sought,
I'll fathom hell or climb to heaven,
And yet esteem that cheap which love has bought.

Fame cannot tempt the bard
Who's famous with his God,
Nor laurel him reward
Who has his Maker's nod.

For I'd rather be thy child
And pupil, in the forest wild,
Than be the king of men elsewhere,
And most sovereign slave of care:
To have one moment of thy dawn,
Than share the city's year forlorn.

SIC VITA

'It is but thin soil where we stand; I have felt my roots in a richer ere this. I have seen a bunch of violets in a glass vase, tied loosely with a straw, which reminded me of myself.'—The Week.

I am a parcel of vain strivings tied
By a chance bond together,
Dangling this way and that, their links
Were made so loose and wide,
Methinks,
For milder weather.

A bunch of violets without their roots,
And sorrel intermixed,
Encircled by a wisp of straw
Once coiled about their shoots,
The law
By which I'm fixed.

A nosegay which Time clutched from out
Those fair Elysian fields,
With weeds and broken stems, in haste,
Doth make the rabble rout
That waste
The day he yields.

And here I bloom for a short hour unseen,
Drinking my juices up,
With no root in the land
To keep my branches green,
But stand
In a bare cup.

Some tender buds were left upon my stem
In mimicry of life,
But ah! the children will not know,
Till time has withered them,

The woe
With which they're rife.

But now I see I was not plucked for nought,
And after in life's vase
Of glass set while I might survive,
But by a kind hand brought
Alive
To a strange place.

THE FISHER'S BOY

My life is like a stroll upon the beach,
As near the ocean's edge as I can go;
My tardy steps its waves sometimes o'erreach,
Sometimes I stay to let them overflow.

My sole employment 'tis, and scrupulous care,
To place my gains beyond the reach of tides,
Each smoother pebble, and each shell more rare,
Which Ocean kindly to my hand confides.

I have but few companions on the shore:
They scorn the strand who sail upon the sea;
Yet oft I think the ocean they've sailed o'er
Is deeper known upon the strand to me.

The middle sea contains no crimson dulse,
Its deeper waves cast up no pearls to view;
Along the shore my hand is on its pulse,
And I converse with many a shipwrecked crew.

THE ATLANTIDES

'The Friend is some fair floating isle of palms eluding the mariner in Pacific Seas.'—The Week.

The smothered streams of love, which flow
More bright than Phlegethon, more low,
Island us ever, like the sea,
In an Atlantic mystery.
Our fabled shores none ever reach,
No mariner has found our beach,
Scarcely our mirage now is seen,
And neighboring waves with floating green,
Yet still the oldest charts contain
Some dotted outline of our main;
In ancient times midsummer days
Unto the western islands' gaze,
To Teneriffe and the Azores,
Have shown our faint and cloud-like shores.

But sink not yet, ye desolate isles,
Anon your coast with commerce smiles,
And richer freights ye'll furnish far
Than Africa or Malabar.
Be fair, be fertile evermore,
Ye rumored but untrodden shore;
Princes and monarchs will contend
Who first unto your lands shall send,
And pawn the jewels of the crown
To call your distant soil their own.

Sea and land are but his neighbors,
And companions in his labors,
Who on the ocean's verge and firm land's end
Doth long and truly seek his Friend.

Many men dwell far inland,
But he alone sits on the strand.
Whether he ponders men or books,
Always still he seaward looks,
Marine news he ever reads,
And the slightest glances heeds,
Feels the sea breeze on his cheek,
At each word the landsmen speak,
In every companion's eye
A sailing vessel doth descry;
In the ocean's sullen roar
From some distant port he hears,
Of wrecks upon a distant shore,
And the ventures of past years.

THE AURORA OF GUIDO

A FRAGMENT

The god of day his car rolls up the slopes,
Reining his prancing steeds with steady hand;
The lingering moon through western shadows gropes,
While Morning sheds its light o'er sea and land.

Castles and cities by the sounding main
Resound with all the busy din of life;
The fisherman unfurls his sails again;
And the recruited warrior bides the strife.

The early breeze ruffles the poplar leaves;
The curling waves reflect the unseen light;
The slumbering sea with the day's impulse heaves,
While o'er the western hill retires the drowsy night.

The seabirds dip their bills in Ocean's foam,
Far circling out over the frothy waves,—

SYMPATHY

Lately, alas! I knew a gentle boy,
Whose features all were cast in Virtue's mould,
As one she had designed for Beauty's toy,
But after manned him for her own stronghold.

On every side he open was as day,
That you might see no lack of strength within;
For walls and ports do only serve alway
For a pretence to feebleness and sin.

Say not that Caesar was victorious,
With toil and strife who stormed the House of Fame;
In other sense this youth was glorious,
Himself a kingdom wheresoe'er he came.

No strength went out to get him victory,
When all was income of its own accord;
For where he went none other was to see,
But all were parcel of their noble lord.

He forayed like the subtle haze of summer,
That stilly shows fresh landscapes to our eyes,
And revolutions works without a murmur,
Or rustling of a leaf beneath the skies.

So was I taken unawares by this,
I quite forgot my homage to confess;
Yet now am forced to know, though hard it is,
I might have loved him, had I loved him less.

Each moment as we nearer drew to each,
A stern respect withheld us farther yet,
So that we seemed beyond each other's reach,
And less acquainted than when first we met.

We two were one while we did sympathise,
So could we not the simplest bargain drive;
And what avails it, now that we are wise,
If absence doth this doubleness contrive?

Eternity may not the chance repeat;
But I must tread my single way alone,
In sad remembrance that we once did meet,
And know that bliss irrevocably gone.

The spheres henceforth my elegy shall sing,
For elegy has other subject none;
Each strain of music in my ears shall ring
Knell of departure from that other one.

Make haste and celebrate my tragedy;
With fitting strain resound, ye woods and fields;
Sorrow is dearer in such case to me
Than all the joys other occasion yields.

Is 't then too late the damage to repair?
Distance, forsooth, from my weak grasp has reft
The empty husk, and clutched the useless tare,
But in my hands the wheat and kernel left.

If I but love that virtue which he is,
Though it be scented in the morning air,
Still shall we be truest acquaintances,

Nor mortals know a sympathy more rare.

FRIENDSHIP

'Friends, Romans, Countrymen, and Lovers.'

Let such pure hate still underprop
Our love, that we may be
Each other's conscience,
And have our sympathy
Mainly from thence.

We'll one another treat like gods,
And all the faith we have
In virtue and in truth, bestow
On either, and suspicion leave
To gods below.

Two solitary stars—
Unmeasured systems far
Between us roll;
But by our conscious light we are
Determined to one pole.

What need confound the sphere?—
Love can afford to wait;
For it no hour 's too late
That witnesseth one duty's end,
Or to another doth beginning lend.

It will subserve no use,
More than the tints of flowers;
Only the independent guest

Frequents its bowers,
Inherits its bequest.

No speech, though kind, has it;
But kinder silence doles
Unto its mates;
By night consoles,
By day congratulates.

What saith the tongue to tongue?
What heareth ear of ear?
By the decrees of fate
From year to year,
Does it communicate.

Pathless the gulf of feeling yawns;
No trivial bridge of words,
Or arch of boldest span,
Can leap the moat that girds
The sincere man.

No show of bolts and bars
Can keep the foeman out,
Or 'scape his secret mine,
Who entered with the doubt
That drew the line.

No warder at the gate
Can let the friendly in;
But, like the sun, o'er all
He will the castle win,
And shine along the wall.

There 's nothing in the world I know

That can escape from love,
For every depth it goes below,
And every height above.

It waits, as waits the sky
Until the clouds go by,
Yet shines serenely on
With an eternal day,
Alike when they are gone,
And when they stay.

Implacable is Love,—
Foes may be bought or teased
From their hostile intent,
But he goes unappeased
Who is on kindness bent.

TRUE KINDNESS

True kindness is a pure divine affinity,
Not founded upon human consanguinity.
It is a spirit, not a blood relation,
Superior to family and station.

TO THE MAIDEN IN THE EAST

Low in the eastern sky
Is set thy glancing eye;
And though its gracious light
Ne'er riseth to my sight,
Yet every star that climbs
Above the gnarled limbs
Of yonder hill,
Conveys thy gentle will.

Believe I knew thy thought,
And that the zephyrs brought
Thy kindest wishes through,
As mine they bear to you;
That some attentive cloud
Did pause amid the crowd
Over my head,
While gentle things were said.

Believe the thrushes sung,
And that the flower-bells rung,
That herbs exhaled their scent,
And beasts knew what was meant,
The trees a welcome waved,
And lakes their margins laved,
When thy free mind
To my retreat did wind.

It was a summer eve,
The air did gently heave
While yet a low-hung cloud
Thy eastern skies did shroud;
The lightning's silent gleam,
Startling my drowsy dream,
Seemed like the flash
Under thy dark eyelash.

From yonder comes the sun,
But soon his course is run,
Rising to trivial day
Along his dusty way;
But thy noontide completes
Only auroral heats,

Nor ever sets,
To hasten vain regrets.

Direct thy pensive eye
Into the western sky;
And when the evening star
Does glimmer from afar
Upon the mountain line,
Accept it for a sign
That I am near,
And thinking of thee here.

I'll be thy Mercury,
Thou Cytherea to me,
Distinguished by thy face
The earth shall learn my place;
As near beneath thy light
Will I outwear the night,
With mingled ray
Leading the westward way.

Still will I strive to be
As if thou wert with me;
Whatever path I take,
It shall be for thy sake,
Of gentle slope and wide,
As thou wert by my side,
Without a root
To trip thy gentle foot.

I'll walk with gentle pace,
And choose the smoothest place,
And careful dip the oar,
And shun the winding shore,

And gently steer my boat
Where water-lilies float,
And cardinal flowers
Stand in their sylvan bowers.

FREE LOVE

My love must be as free
As is the eagle's wing,
Hovering o'er land and sea
And everything.

I must not dim my eye
In thy saloon,
I must not leave my sky
And nightly moon.

Be not the fowler's net
Which stays my flight,
And craftily is set
T' allure the sight.

But be the favoring gale
That bears me on,
And still doth fill my sail
When thou art gone.

I cannot leave my sky
For thy caprice,
True love would soar as high
As heaven is.

The eagle would not brook
Her mate thus won,

Who trained his eye to look
Beneath the sun.

RUMORS FROM AN ÆOLIAN HARP

There is a vale which none hath seen,
Where foot of man has never been,
Such as here lives with toil and strife,
An anxious and a sinful life.

There every virtue has its birth,
Ere it descends upon the earth,
And thither every deed returns,
Which in the generous bosom burns.

There love is warm, and youth is young,
And poetry is yet unsung,
For Virtue still adventures there,
And freely breathes her native air.

And ever, if you hearken well,
You still may hear its vesper bell,
And tread of high-souled men go by,
Their thoughts conversing with the sky.

LINES

Though all the Fates should prove unkind,
Leave not your native land behind.
The ship, becalmed, at length stands still;
The steed must rest beneath the hill;
But swiftly still our fortunes pace
To find us out in every place.

The vessel, though her masts be firm,
Beneath her copper bears a worm;
Around the Cape, across the Line,
Till fields of ice her course confine;
It matters not how smooth the breeze,
How shallow or how deep the seas,
Whether she bears Manilla twine,
Or in her hold Madeira wine,
Or China teas, or Spanish hides,
In port or quarantine she rides;
Far from New England's blustering shore,
New England's worm her hulk shall bore,
And sink her in the Indian seas,—
Twine, wine, and hides, and China teas.

'Before each van
Prick forth the aery knights, and couch their spears
Till thickest legions close; with feats of arms
From either end of Heaven the welkin burns.'
Away! away! away! away!
Ye have not kept your secret well,
I will abide that other day,
Those other lands ye tell.

Has time no leisure left for these,
The acts that ye rehearse?
Is not eternity a lease
For better deeds than verse?

'Tis sweet to hear of heroes dead,
To know them still alive,
But sweeter if we earn their bread,
And in us they survive.

Our life should feed the springs of fame
With a perennial wave,
As ocean feeds the babbling founts
Which find in it their grave.

Ye skies drop gently round my breast,
And be my corslet blue,
Ye earth receive my lance in rest,
My faithful charger you;

Ye stars my spear-heads in the sky,
My arrow-tips ye are;
I see the routed foemen fly,
My bright spears fixèd are.

Give me an angel for a foe,
Fix now the place and time,
And straight to meet him I will go
Above the starry chime.

And with our clashing bucklers' clang
The heavenly spheres shall ring,
While bright the northern lights shall hang
Beside our tourneying.

And if she lose her champion true,
Tell Heaven not despair,
For I will be her champion new,
Her fame I will repair.

A RIVER SCENE

The river swelleth more and more,
Like some sweet influence stealing o'er

The passive town; and for a while
Each tussock makes a tiny isle,
Where, on some friendly Ararat,
Resteth the weary water-rat.

No ripple shows Musketaquid,
Her very current e'en is hid,
As deepest souls do calmest rest,
When thoughts are swelling in the breast,
And she that in the summer's drought
Doth make a rippling and a rout,
Sleeps from Nahshawtuck to the Cliff,
Unruffled by a single skiff.
But by a thousand distant hills
The louder roar a thousand rills,
And many a spring which now is dumb,
And many a stream with smothered hum,
Doth swifter well and faster glide,
Though buried deep beneath the tide.

Our village shows a rural Venice,
Its broad lagoons where yonder fen is;
As lovely as the Bay of Naples
Yon placid cove amid the maples;
And in my neighbour's field of corn
I recognise the Golden Horn.

Here Nature taught from year to year,
When only red men came to hear;
Methinks 'twas in this school of art
Venice and Naples learned their part,
But still their mistress, to my mind,
Her young disciples leaves behind.

RIVER SONG

Ply the oars! away! away!
In each dew-drop of the morning
Lies the promise of a day.

Rivers from the sunrise flow,
Springing with the dewy morn;
Voyageurs 'gainst time do row,
Idle noon nor sunset know,
Ever even with the dawn.

• • • • • •

Since that first 'Away! away!'
Many a lengthy reach we 've rowed,
Still the sparrow on the spray
Hastes to usher in the day
With her simple-stanza'd ode.

SOME TUMULTUOUS LITTLE RILL

Some tumultuous little rill,
Purling round its storied pebble,
Tinkling to the selfsame tune,
From September until June,
Which no drought doth e'er enfeeble.

Silent flows the parent stream,
And if rocks do lie below,
Smothers with her waves the din,
As it were a youthful sin,
Just as still, and just as slow.

BOAT SONG

Thus, perchance, the Indian hunter,
Many a lagging year agone,
Gliding o'er thy rippling waters,
Lowly hummed a natural song.

Now the sun 's behind the willows,
Now he gleams along the waves,
Faintly o'er the wearied billows
Come the spirits of the braves.

TO MY BROTHER

Brother, where dost thou dwell?
What sun shines for thee now?
Dost thou indeed fare well,
As we wished thee here below?

What season didst thou find?
'Twas winter here.
Are not the Fates more kind
Than they appear?

Is thy brow clear again
As in thy youthful years?
And was that ugly pain
The summit of thy fears?

Yet thou wast cheery still;
They could not quench thy fire;
Thou didst abide their will,
And then retire.

Where chiefly shall I look

To feel thy presence near?
Along the neighboring brook
May I thy voice still hear?

Dost thou still haunt the brink
Of yonder river's tide?
And may I ever think
That thou art by my side?

What bird wilt thou employ
To bring me word of thee?
For it would give them joy—
'Twould give them liberty—
To serve their former lord
With wing and minstrelsy.

A sadder strain mixed with their song,
They 've slowlier built their nests;
Since thou art gone
Their lively labor rests.

Where is the finch, the thrush,
I used to hear?
Ah, they could well abide
The dying year.

Now they no more return,
I hear them not;
They have remained to mourn,
Or else forgot.

STANZAS

Nature doth have her dawn each day,

But mine are far between;
Content, I cry, for, sooth to say,
Mine brightest are, I ween.

For when my sun doth deign to rise,
Though it be her noontide,
Her fairest field in shadow lies,
Nor can my light abide.

Sometimes I bask me in her day,
Conversing with my mate,
But if we interchange one ray,
Forthwith her heats abate.

Through his discourse I climb and see
As from some eastern hill,
A brighter morrow rise to me
Than lieth in her skill.

As 'twere two summer days in one,
Two Sundays come together,
Our rays united make one sun,
With fairest summer weather.

THE INWARD MORNING

Packed in my mind lie all the clothes
Which outward nature wears,
And in its fashion's hourly change
It all things else repairs.

In vain I look for change abroad,
And can no difference find,
Till some new ray of peace uncalled

Illumes my inmost mind.

What is it gilds the trees and clouds,
And paints the heavens so gay,
But yonder fast-abiding light
With its unchanging ray?

Lo, when the sun streams through the wood,
Upon a winter's morn,
Where'er his silent beams intrude
The murky night is gone.

How could the patient pine have known
The morning breeze would come,
Or humble flowers anticipate
The insect's noonday hum,—

Till the new light with morning cheer
From far streamed through the aisles,
And nimbly told the forest trees
For many stretching miles?

I've heard within my inmost soul
Such cheerful morning news,
In the horizon of my mind
Have seen such orient hues,

As in the twilight of the dawn,
When the first birds awake,
Are heard within some silent wood,
Where they the small twigs break,

Or in the eastern skies are seen,
Before the sun appears,

The harbingers of summer heats
Which from afar he bears.

GREECE

When life contracts into a vulgar span,
And human nature tires to be a man,
I thank the Gods for Greece,
That permanent realm of peace.
For as the rising moon far in the night
Chequers the shade with her forerunning light,
So in my darkest hour my senses seem
To catch from her Acropolis a gleam.

Greece, who am I that should remember thee,
Thy Marathon, and thy Thermopylae?
Is my life vulgar, my fate mean,
Which on such golden memories can lean?

THE FUNERAL BELL

One more is gone
Out of the busy throng
That tread these paths;
The church-bell tolls,
Its sad knell rolls
To many hearths.

Flower-bells toll not,
Their echoes roll not
Upon my ear;
There still perchance
That gentle spirit haunts
A fragrant bier.

Low lies the pall,
Lowly the mourners all
Their passage grope;
No sable hue
Mars the serene blue
Of heaven's cope.

In distant dell
Faint sounds the funeral bell;
A heavenly chime;
Some poet there
Weaves the light-burthened air
Into sweet rhyme.

THE SUMMER RAIN

My books I 'd fain cast off, I cannot read,
'Twixt every page my thoughts go stray at large
Down in the meadow, where is richer feed,
And will not mind to hit their proper targe.

Plutarch was good, and so was Homer too,
Our Shakespeare's life were rich to live again,
What Plutarch read, that was not good nor true,
Nor Shakespeare's books, unless his books were men.

Here while I lie beneath this walnut bough,
What care I for the Greeks or for Troy town,
If juster battles are enacted now
Between the ants upon this hummock's crown?

Bid Homer wait till I the issue learn,
If red or black the gods will favor most,

Or yonder Ajax will the phalanx turn,
Struggling to heave some rock against the host.

Tell Shakespeare to attend some leisure hour,
For now I've business with this drop of dew,
And see you not, the clouds prepare a shower,—
I 'll meet him shortly when the sky is blue.

This bed of herdsgrass and wild oats was spread
Last year with nicer skill than monarchs use,
A clover tuft is pillow for my head,
And violets quite overtop my shoes.

And now the cordial clouds have shut all in,
And gently swells the wind to say all 's well;
The scattered drops are falling fast and thin,
Some in the pool, some in the flower-bell.

I am well drenched upon my bed of oats;
But see that globe come rolling down its stem,
Now like a lonely planet there it floats,
And now it sinks into my garment's hem.

Drip, drip the trees for all the country round,
And richness rare distils from every bough;
The wind alone it is makes every sound,
Shaking down crystals on the leaves below.

For shame the sun will never show himself,
Who could not with his beams e'er melt me so;
My dripping locks,—they would become an elf,
Who in a beaded coat does gayly go.

MIST

Low-anchored cloud,
Newfoundland air,
Fountain-head and source of rivers,
Dew-cloth, dream-drapery,
And napkin spread by fays;
Drifting meadow of the air,
Where bloom the daisied banks and violets,
And in whose fenny labyrinth
The bittern booms and heron wades;
Spirit of lakes and seas and rivers,—
Bear only perfumes and the scent
Of healing herbs to just men's fields.

SMOKE

Light-winged Smoke, Icarian bird,
Melting thy pinions in thy upward flight;
Lark without song, and messenger of dawn,
Circling above the hamlets as thy nest;
Or else, departing dream, and shadowy form
Of midnight vision, gathering up thy skirts;
By night star-veiling, and by day
Darkening the light and blotting out the sun;
Go thou, my incense, upward from this hearth,
And ask the gods to pardon this clear flame.

HAZE

Woof of the sun,[1] ethereal gauze,
Woven of Nature's richest stuffs,
Visible heat, air-water, and dry sea,
Last conquest of the eye;
Toil of the day displayed, sun-dust,

Aerial surf upon the shores of earth,
Ethereal estuary, frith of light,
Breakers of air, billows of heat,
Fine summer spray on inland seas;
Bird of the sun, transparent-winged,
Owlet of noon, soft-pinioned,
From heath or stubble rising without song,—
Establish thy serenity o'er the fields.

THE MOON

'Time wears her not; she doth his chariot guide;
Mortality below her orb is placed.'—Raleigh.

The full-orbed moon with unchanged ray
Mounts up the eastern sky,
Not doomed to these short nights for aye,
But shining steadily.

She does not wane, but my fortùne,
Which her rays do not bless;
My wayward path declineth soon,
But she shines not the less.

And if she faintly glimmers here
And palèd is her light,
Yet always in her proper sphere
She's mistress of the night.

THE VIREO

Upon the lofty elm-tree sprays
The vireo rings the changes sweet,
During the trivial summer days,
Striving to lift our thoughts above the street.

THE POET'S DELAY

In vain I see the morning rise,
In vain observe the western blaze,
Who idly look to other skies,
Expecting life by other ways.

Amidst such boundless wealth without,
I only still am poor within,
The birds have sung their summer out,
But still my spring does not begin.

Shall I then wait the autumn wind,
Compelled to seek a milder day,
And leave no curious nest behind,
No woods still echoing to my lay?

LINES

All things are current found
On earthly ground,
Spirits and elements
Have their descents.

Night and day, year on year,
High and low, far and near,

These are our own aspects,
These are our own regrets.
Ye gods of the shore,
Who abide evermore,
I see your far headland,
Stretching on either hand;

I hear the sweet evening sounds
From your undecaying grounds;
Cheat me no more with time,
Take me to your clime.

NATURE'S CHILD

I am the autumnal sun,
With autumn gales my race is run;
When will the hazel put forth its flowers,
Or the grape ripen under my bowers?
When will the harvest or the hunter's moon,
Turn my midnight into mid-noon?
I am all sere and yellow,
And to my core mellow.
The mast is dropping within my woods,
The winter is lurking within my moods,
And the rustling of the withered leaf
Is the constant music of my grief.

THE FALL OF THE LEAF

Thank God who seasons thus the year,
And sometimes kindly slants his rays;
For in his winter he's most near
And plainest seen upon the shortest days.

Who gently tempers now his heats,
And then his harsher cold, lest we
Should surfeit on the summer's sweets,
Or pine upon the winter's crudity.

A sober mind will walk alone,

Apart from nature, if need be,
And only its own seasons own;
For nature leaving its humanity.

Sometimes a late autumnal thought
Has crossed my mind in green July,
And to its early freshness brought
Late ripened fruits, and an autumnal sky.

The evening of the year draws on,
The fields a later aspect wear;
Since Summer's garishness is gone,
Some grains of night tincture the noontide air.

Behold! the shadows of the trees
Now circle wider 'bout their stem,
Like sentries that by slow degrees
Perform their rounds, gently protecting them.

And as the year doth decline,
The sun allows a scantier light;
Behind each needle of the pine
There lurks a small auxiliar to the night.

I hear the cricket's slumbrous lay
Around, beneath me, and on high;
It rocks the night, it soothes the day,
And everywhere is Nature's lullaby.

But most he chirps beneath the sod,
When he has made his winter bed;
His creak grown fainter but more broad,
A film of autumn o'er the summer spread.

Small birds, in fleets migrating by,
Now beat across some meadow's bay,
And as they tack and veer on high,
With faint and hurried click beguile the way.

Far in the woods, these golden days,
Some leaf obeys its Maker's call;
And through their hollow aisles it plays
With delicate touch the prelude of the Fall.

Gently withdrawing from its stem,
It lightly lays itself along
Where the same hand hath pillowed them,
Resigned to sleep upon the old year's throng.

The loneliest birch is brown and sere,
The furthest pool is strewn with leaves,
Which float upon their watery bier,
Where is no eye that sees, no heart that grieves.

The jay screams through the chestnut wood;
The crisped and yellow leaves around
Are hue and texture of my mood—
And these rough burrs my heirlooms on the ground.

The threadbare trees, so poor and thin—
They are no wealthier than I;
But with as brave a core within
They rear their boughs to the October sky.

Poor knights they are which bravely wait
The charge of Winter's cavalry,
Keeping a simple Roman state,
Discumbered of their Persian luxury.

SMOKE IN WINTER

The sluggish smoke curls up from some deep dell,
The stiffened air exploring in the dawn,
And making slow acquaintance with the day;
Delaying now upon its heavenward course,
In wreathed loiterings dallying with itself,
With as uncertain purpose and slow deed,
As its half-wakened master by the hearth,
Whose mind, still slumbering, and sluggish thoughts
Have not yet swept into the onward current
Of the new day;—and now it streams afar,
The while the chopper goes with step direct,
And mind intent to wield the early axe.

First in the dusky dawn he sends abroad
His early scout, his emissary, smoke,
The earliest, latest pilgrim from the roof,
To feel the frosty air, inform the day;
And while he crouches still beside the hearth,
Nor musters courage to unbar the door,
It has gone down the glen with the light wind,
And o'er the plain unfurled its venturous wreath,
Draped the tree-tops, loitered upon the hill,
And warmed the pinions of the early bird;
And now, perchance, high in the crispy air,
Has caught sight of the day o'er the earth's edge,
And greets its master's eye at his low door,
As some refulgent cloud in the upper sky.

WINTER MEMORIES

Within the circuit of this plodding life

There enter moments of an azure hue,
Untarnished fair as is the violet
Or anemone, when the spring strews them
By some meandering rivulet, which make
The best philosophy untrue that aims
But to console man for his grievances.
I have remembered when the winter came,
High in my chamber in the frosty nights,
When in the still light of the cheerful moon,
On every twig and rail and jutting spout,
The icy spears were adding to their length
Against the arrows of the coming sun,—
How in the shimmering noon of summer past
Some unrecorded beam slanted across
The upland pastures where the johnswort grew;
Or heard, amid the verdure of my mind,
The bee's long smothered hum, on the blue flag
Loitering amidst the mead; or busy rill,
Which now through all its course stands still and dumb,
Its own memorial,—purling at its play
Along the slopes, and through the meadows next,
Until its youthful sound was hushed at last
In the staid current of the lowland stream;
Or seen the furrows shine but late upturned,
And where the fieldfare followed in the rear,
When all the fields around lay bound and hoar
Beneath a thick integument of snow:—
So by God's cheap economy made rich,
To go upon my winter's task again.

STANZAS WRITTEN AT WALDEN

When Winter fringes every bough
With his fantastic wreath,

And puts the seal of silence now
Upon the leaves beneath;

When every stream in its pent-house
Goes gurgling on its way,
And in his gallery the mouse
Nibbleth the meadow hay;

Methinks the summer still is nigh,
And lurketh underneath,
As that same meadow-mouse doth lie
Snug in that last year's heath.

And if perchance the chicadee
Lisp a faint note anon,
The snow is summer's canopy,
Which she herself put on.

Fair blossoms deck the cheerful trees,
And dazzling fruits depend;
The north wind sighs a summer breeze,
The nipping frosts to fend,

Bringing glad tidings unto me,
The while I stand all ear,
Of a serene eternity,
Which need not winter fear.

Out on the silent pond straightway
The restless ice doth crack,
And pond-sprites merry gambols play
Amid the deafening rack.

Eager I hasten to the vale,

As if I heard brave news,
How Nature held high festival,
Which it were hard to lose.

I gambol with my neighbor ice,
And sympathising quake,
As each new crack darts in a trice
Across the gladsome lake.

One with the cricket in the ground,
And fagot on the hearth,
Resounds the rare domestic sound
Along the forest path.

THE THAW

I saw the civil sun drying earth's tears,
Her tears of joy that only faster flowed.

Fain would I stretch me by the highway side
To thaw and trickle with the melting snow;
That mingled, soul and body, with the tide,
I too may through the pores of nature flow.

A WINTER SCENE

The rabbit leaps,
The mouse out-creeps,
The flag out-peeps
Beside the brook;
The ferret weeps,
The marmot sleeps,
The owlet keeps
In his snug nook.

The apples thaw,
The ravens caw,
The squirrels gnaw
The frozen fruit.
To their retreat
I track the feet
Of mice that eat
The apple's root.

The snow-dust falls,
The otter crawls,
The partridge calls,
Far in the wood.
The traveller dreams,
The tree-ice gleams,
The blue-jay screams
In angry mood.

The willows droop,
The alders stoop,
The pheasants group
Beneath the snow.
The catkins green
Cast o'er the scene
A summer's sheen,
A genial glow.

THE CROW

Thou dusky spirit of the wood,
Bird of an ancient brood,
Flitting thy lonely way,
A meteor in the summer's day,

From wood to wood, from hill to hill,
Low over forest, field, and rill,
What wouldst thou say?
Why shouldst thou haunt the day?
What makes thy melancholy float?
What bravery inspires thy throat,
And bears thee up above the clouds,
Over desponding human crowds,
Which far below
Lay thy haunts low?

TO A STRAY FOWL

Poor bird! destined to lead thy life
Far in the adventurous west,
And here to be debarred to-night
From thy accustomed nest;
Must thou fall back upon old instinct now—
Well-nigh extinct under man's fickle care?
Did heaven bestow its quenchless inner light
So long ago, for thy small want to-night?
Why stand'st upon thy toes to crow so late?
The moon is deaf to thy low feathered fate;
Or dost thou think so to possess the night,
And people the drear dark with thy brave sprite?
And now with anxious eye thou look'st about,
While the relentless shade draws on its veil,
For some sure shelter from approaching dews,
And the insidious step of nightly foes.
I fear imprisonment has dulled thy wit,
Or ingrained servitude extinguished it—
But no—dim memory of the days of yore,
By Brahmapootra and the Jumna's shore,
Where thy proud race flew swiftly o'er the heath,

And sought its food the jungle's shade beneath,
Has taught thy wings to seek yon friendly trees,
As erst by Indus' bank and far Ganges.

MOUNTAINS

With frontier strength ye stand your ground,
With grand content ye circle round,
Tumultuous silence for all sound,
Ye distant nursery of rills,
Monadnock, and the Peterborough hills;—
Firm argument that never stirs,
Outcircling the philosophers,—
Like some vast fleet
Sailing through rain and sleet,
Through winter's cold and summer's heat;
Still holding on upon your high emprise,
Until ye find a shore amid the skies;
Not skulking close to land,
With cargo contraband;
For they who sent a venture out by ye
Have set the Sun to see
Their honesty.
Ships of the line, each one,
Ye westward run,
Convoying clouds,
Which cluster in your shrouds,
Always before the gale,
Under a press of sail,
With weight of metal all untold;—
I seem to feel ye in my firm seat here,
Immeasurable depth of hold,
And breadth of beam, and length of running gear.

Methinks ye take luxurious pleasure
In your novel western leisure;
So cool your brows and freshly blue,
As Time had nought for ye to do;
For ye lie at your length,
An unappropriated strength,
Unhewn primeval timber
For knees so stiff, for masts so limber,
The stock of which new earths are made,
One day to be our western trade,
Fit for the stanchions of a world
Which through the seas of space is hurled.

While we enjoy a lingering ray,
Ye still o'ertop the western day,
Reposing yonder on God's croft,
Like solid stacks of hay.
So bold a line as ne'er was writ
On any page by human wit;
The forest glows as if
An enemy's camp-fires shone
Along the horizon,
Or the day's funeral pyre
Were lighted there;
Edged with silver and with gold,
The clouds hang o'er in damask fold,
And with fresh depth of amber light
The west is dight,
Where still a few rays slant,
That even Heaven seems extravagant.
Watatic Hill
Lies on the horizon's sill
Like a child's toy left overnight,
And other duds to left and right;

On the earth's edge, mountains and trees
Stand as they were on air graven,
Or as the vessels in a haven
Await the morning breeze.
I fancy even
Through your defiles windeth the way to heaven;
And yonder still, in spite of history's page,
Linger the golden and the silver age;
Upon the laboring gale
The news of future centuries is brought,
And of new dynasties of thought,
From your remotest vale.

But special I remember thee,
Wachusett, who like me
Standest alone without society.
Thy far blue eye,
A remnant of the sky,
Seen through the clearing of the gorge,
Or from the windows of the forge,
Doth leaven all it passes by.
Nothing is true,
But stands 'tween me and you,
Thou western pioneer,
Who know'st not shame nor fear,
By venturous spirit driven
Under the eaves of heaven,
And canst expand thee there,
And breathe enough of air.
Even beyond the West
Thou migratest
Into unclouded tracts,
Without a pilgrim's axe,

Cleaving thy road on high
With thy well-tempered brow,
And mak'st thyself a clearing in the sky.
Upholding heaven, holding down earth,
Thy pastime from thy birth,
Not steadied by the one, nor leaning on the other;—
May I approve myself thy worthy brother!

THE RESPECTABLE FOLKS

The respectable folks,—
Where dwell they?
They whisper in the oaks,
And they sigh in the hay;
Summer and winter, night and day,
Out on the meadow, there dwell they.
They never die,
Nor snivel, nor cry,
Nor ask our pity
With a wet eye.
A sound estate they ever mend,
To every asker readily lend;
To the ocean wealth,
To the meadow health,
To Time his length,
To the rocks strength,
To the stars light,
To the weary night,
To the busy day,
To the idle play;
And so their good cheer never ends,
For all are their debtors, and all their friends.

POVERTY

If I am poor,
It is that I am proud;
If God has made me naked and a boor,
He did not think it fit his work to shroud.

The poor man comes direct from heaven to earth,
As stars drop down the sky, and tropic beams;
The rich receives in our gross air his birth,
As from low suns are slanted golden gleams.

Yon sun is naked, bare of satellite,
Unless our earth and moon that office hold;
Though his perpetual day feareth no night,
And his perennial summer dreads no cold.

Mankind may delve, but cannot my wealth spend;
If I no partial wealth appropriate,
No armèd ships unto the Indies send,
None robs me of my Orient estate.

PILGRIMS

'Have you not seen
In ancient times
Pilgrims pass by
Toward other climes?
With shining faces,
Youthful and strong,
Mounting this hill
With speech and with song?'

'Ah, my good sir,
I know not those ways:

Little my knowledge,
Tho' many my days.
When I have slumbered,
I have heard sounds
As of travellers passing
These my grounds:

''Twas a sweet music
Wafted them by,
I could not tell
If afar off or nigh.
Unless I dreamed it,
This was of yore:
I never told it
To mortal before;

'Never remembered
But in my dreams,
What to me waking
A miracle seems.'

CONSCIENCE

Conscience is instinct bred in the house,
Feeling and Thinking propagate the sin
By an unnatural breeding in and in.
I say, Turn it out doors,
Into the moors.
I love a life whose plot is simple,
And does not thicken with every pimple,
A soul so sound no sickly conscience binds it,
That makes the universe no worse than 't finds it.
I love an earnest soul,
Whose mighty joy and sorrow

Are not drowned in a bowl,
And brought to life to-morrow
That lives one tragedy,
And not seventy;
A conscience worth keeping,
Laughing not weeping;
A conscience wise and steady,
And for ever ready;
Not changing with events,
Dealing in compliments;
A conscience exercised about
Large things, where one may doubt.
I love a soul not all of wood,
Predestinated to be good,
But true to the backbone
Unto itself alone,
And false to none;
Born to its own affairs,
Its own joys and own cares;
By whom the work which God begun
Is finished, and not undone;
Taken up where he left off,
Whether to worship or to scoff;
If not good, why then evil,
If not good god, good devil.
Goodness!—you hypocrite, come out of that,
Live your life, do your work, then take your hat.
I have no patience towards
Such conscientious cowards.
Give me simple laboring folk,
Who love their work,
Whose virtue is a song
To cheer God along.

That stock thus thinned will soon redeem its hours,
And by another year,
Such as God knows, with freer air,
More fruits and fairer flowers
Will bear,
While I droop here.

THE DEPARTURE

In this roadstead I have ridden,
In this covert I have hidden;
Friendly thoughts were cliffs to me,
And I hid beneath their lea.

This true people took the stranger,
And warm-hearted housed the ranger;
They received their roving guest,
And have fed him with the best;

Whatsoe'er the land afforded
To the stranger's wish accorded;
Shook the olive, stripped the vine,
And expressed the strengthening wine.

And by night they did spread o'er him
What by day they spread before him;—
That good-will which was repast
Was his covering at last.

The stranger moored him to their pier
Without anxiety or fear;
By day he walked the sloping land,
By night the gentle heavens he scanned.

When first his barque stood inland
To the coast of that far Finland,
Sweet-watered brooks came tumbling to the shore
The weary mariner to restore.

And still he stayed from day to day,
If he their kindness might repay;
But more and more
The sullen waves came rolling toward the shore.

And still the more the stranger waited,
The less his argosy was freighted,
And still the more he stayed,
The less his debt was paid.

So he unfurled his shrouded mast
To receive the fragrant blast;
And that same refreshing gale
Which had wooed him to remain
Again and again,
It was that filled his sail
And drove him to the main.

All day the low-hung clouds
Dropt tears into the sea;
And the wind amid the shrouds
Sighed plaintively.

INDEPENDENCE

My life more civil is and free
Than any civil polity.

Ye princes, keep your realms

And circumscribèd power,
Not wide as are my dreams,
Nor rich as is this hour.

What can ye give which I have not?
What can ye take which I have got?
Can ye defend the dangerless?
Can ye inherit nakedness?

To all true wants Time's ear is deaf,
Penurious States lend no relief
Out of their pelf:
But a free soul—thank God—
Can help itself.

Be sure your fate
Doth keep apart its state,—
Not linked with any band,
Even the noblest in the land,—

In tented fields with cloth of gold
No place doth hold,
But is more chivalrous than they are,
And sigheth for a nobler war;
A finer strain its trumpet rings,
A brighter gleam its armor flings.

The life that I aspire to live,
No man proposeth me;
No trade upon the street[2]
Wears its emblazonry.

DING DONG

When the world grows old by the chimney-side,
Then forth to the youngling nooks I glide,
Where over the water and over the land
The bells are booming on either hand.

Now up they go ding, then down again dong,
And awhile they ring to the same old song,
For the metal goes round at a single bound,
A-cutting the fields with its measured sound,
While the tired tongue falls with a lengthened boom
As solemn and loud as the crack of doom.

Then changed is their measure to tone upon tone,
And seldom it is that one sound comes alone,
For they ring out their peals in a mingled throng,
And the breezes waft the loud ding-dong along.

When the echo hath reached me in this lone vale,
I am straightway a hero in coat of mail,
I tug at my belt and I march on my post,
And feel myself more than a match for a host.

MY PRAYER

Great God, I ask thee for no meaner pelf
Than that I may not disappoint myself;
That in my action I may soar as high
As I can now discern with this clear eye.

And next in value, which thy kindness lends,
That I may greatly disappoint my friends,
Howe'er they think or hope that it may be,
They may not dream how thou 'st distinguished me.

That my weak hand may equal my firm faith,
And my life practise more than my tongue saith;
That my low conduct may not show,
Nor my relenting lines,
That I thy purpose did not know,
Or overrated thy designs.

Henry David Thoreau

Henry David Thoreau (see name pronunciation; July 12, 1817 – May 6, 1862) was an American author, poet, philosopher, abolitionist, naturalist, tax resister, development critic, surveyor, and historian. A leading transcendentalist,[2] Thoreau is best known for his book Walden, a reflection upon simple living in natural surroundings, and his essay Resistance to Civil Government (also known as Civil Disobedience), an argument for disobedience to an unjust state.

Thoreau's books, articles, essays, journals, and poetry total over 20 volumes. Among his lasting contributions are his writings on natural history and philosophy, where he anticipated the methods and findings of ecology and environmental history, two sources of modern-day environmentalism. His literary style interweaves close natural observation, personal experience, pointed rhetoric, symbolic meanings, and historical lore, while displaying a poetic sensibility, philosophical austerity, and "Yankee" love of practical detail.[3] He was also deeply interested in the idea of survival in the face of hostile elements, historical change, and natural decay; at the same time he advocated abandoning waste and illusion in order to discover life's true essential needs.[3]

He was a lifelong abolitionist, delivering lectures that attacked the Fugitive Slave Law while praising the writings of Wendell Phillips and defending abolitionist John Brown. Thoreau's philosophy of civil disobedience later influenced the political thoughts and actions of such notable figures as Leo Tolstoy, Mahatma Gandhi, and Martin Luther King, Jr.

Thoreau is sometimes cited as an anarchist.[4] Though Civil Disobedience seems to call for improving rather than abolishing government — "I ask for, not at once no government, but at once a better government"[5] — the direction of this improvement points toward anarchism: "'That government is best which governs not at all;' and when men are prepared for it, that will be the kind of government which they will have."[5] Richard T. Drinnon partly blames Thoreau for the ambiguity, noting that Thoreau's "sly satire, his liking for wide margins for his writing, and his fondness for paradox provided ammunition for widely divergent interpretations of 'Civil Disobedience'."[6]

Name pronunciation and physical appearance

Amos Bronson Alcott and Thoreau's aunt each wrote that "Thoreau" is pronounced like the word "thorough" (pronounced THUR-oh—/ˈθʌroʊ/—in General American,[7][8] but more precisely THOR-oh—/ˈθɔːroʊ/—in 19th-century New England). Edward Waldo Emerson wrote that the name should be pronounced "Thó-row", with the h sounded and stress on the first syllable.[9] Among modern-day American speakers, it is perhaps more commonly pronounced thə-ROH—/θəˈroʊ/—with stress on the second syllable.[10][11]

In appearance he was homely, with a nose that he called "my most prominent feature."[12] Of his face and disposition, Ellery Channing wrote: "His face, once seen, could not be forgotten. The features were quite marked: the nose aquiline or very Roman, like one of the portraits of Caesar (more like a beak, as was said); large overhanging brows above the deepest set blue eyes that could be seen, in certain lights, and in others gray, — eyes expressive of all shades of feeling, but never weak or near-sighted; the forehead not unusually broad or high, full of concentrated energy and purpose; the mouth with prominent lips, pursed up with meaning and thought when silent, and giving out when open with the most varied and unusual instructive sayings."[13]

Life

Early life and education, 1817–1836

Henry David Thoreau was born David Henry Thoreau[14] in Concord, Massachusetts, into the "modest New England family"[15] of John Thoreau (a pencil maker) and Cynthia Dunbar. His paternal grandfather was born in Jersey.[16] His maternal grandfather, Asa Dunbar, led Harvard's 1766 student "Butter Rebellion",[17] the first recorded student protest in the Colonies.[18] David Henry was named after a recently deceased paternal uncle, David Thoreau. He did not become "Henry David" until after college, although he never petitioned to make a legal name change.[19] He had two older siblings, Helen and John Jr., and a younger sister, Sophia.[20] Thoreau's birthplace still exists on Virginia Road in Concord. The house has recently been restored by the Thoreau Farm Trust,[21] a nonprofit organization, and is now open to the public.

He studied at Harvard College between 1833 and 1837. He lived in Hollis Hall and took courses in rhetoric, classics, philosophy, mathematics, and science.[citation needed] He was a member of the Institute of 1770[22] (now the Hasty Pudding Club). A legend proposes that Thoreau refused to pay the five-dollar fee for a Harvard diploma. In fact, the master's degree he declined to purchase had no academic merit: Harvard College offered it to graduates "who proved their physical worth by being alive three years after graduating, and their saving, earning, or inheriting quality or condition by having Five Dollars to give the college."[23] His comment was: "Let every sheep keep its own skin",[24] a reference to the tradition of diplomas being written on sheepskin vellum.

Return to Concord, 1836–1842

The traditional professions open to college graduates—law, the church, business, medicine—failed to interest Thoreau,[25]:25 so in 1835 he took a leave of absence from Harvard, during which he taught school in Canton, Massachusetts. After he graduated in 1837, he joined the faculty of the Concord public school, but resigned after a few weeks rather than administer corporal punishment.[25]:25 He and his brother John then opened a grammar school in Concord in 1838 called Concord Academy.[25]:25 They introduced several progressive concepts, including nature walks and visits to local shops and businesses. The school ended when John became fatally ill from tetanus in 1842 after cutting himself while shaving.[26][27] He died in his brother Henry's arms.[28]

Upon graduation Thoreau returned home to Concord, where he met Ralph Waldo Emerson through a mutual friend.[15] Emerson took a paternal and at times patronizing interest in Thoreau, advising the young man and introducing him to a circle of local writers and thinkers, including Ellery Channing, Margaret Fuller, Bronson Alcott, Nathaniel Hawthorne and his son Julian Hawthorne, who was a boy at the time.

Emerson urged Thoreau to contribute essays and poems to a quarterly periodical, The Dial, and Emerson lobbied editor Margaret Fuller to publish those writings. Thoreau's first essay published there was Aulus Persius Flaccus, an essay on the playwright of the same name, published in The Dial in July 1840.[29] It consisted of revised passages from his journal, which he had begun keeping at Emerson's suggestion. The first journal entry on October 22, 1837, reads, "'What are you doing now?' he asked. 'Do you keep a journal?' So I make my first entry to-day."[30]

Thoreau was a philosopher of nature and its relation to the human condition. In his early years he followed Transcendentalism, a loose and eclectic idealist philosophy advocated by Emerson, Fuller, and Alcott. They held that an ideal spiritual state transcends, or goes beyond, the physical and empirical, and that one achieves that insight via personal intuition rather than religious doctrine. In their view, Nature is the outward sign of inward spirit, expressing the "radical correspondence of visible things and human thoughts", as Emerson wrote in Nature (1836).

On April 18, 1841, Thoreau moved into the Emerson house.[31] There, from 1841–1844, he served as the children's tutor, editorial assistant, and repair man/gardener. For a few months in 1843, he moved to the home of William Emerson on Staten Island,[32] and tutored the family sons while seeking contacts among literary men and journalists in the city who might help publish his writings, including his future literary representative Horace Greeley.[33]:68

Thoreau returned to Concord and worked in his family's pencil factory, which he continued to do for most of his adult life. He rediscovered the process to make a good pencil out of inferior graphite by using clay as the binder; this invention improved upon graphite found in New Hampshire and bought in 1821 by relative Charles Dunbar. (The process of mixing graphite and clay, known as the Conté process, was patented by Nicolas-Jacques Conté in 1795). His other source had been Tantiusques, an Indian operated mine in Sturbridge, Massachusetts. Later, Thoreau converted the factory to produce plumbago (graphite), which was used to ink typesetting machines.[34]

Once back in Concord, Thoreau went through a restless period. In April 1844 he and his friend Edward Hoar accidentally set a fire that consumed 300 acres (1.2 km2) of Walden Woods.[35]

Civil Disobedience and the Walden years, 1845–1849

I went to the woods because I wished to live deliberately, to front only the essential facts of life, and see if I could not learn what it had to teach, and not, when I came to die, discover that I had not lived. I did not wish to live what was not life, living is so dear; nor did I wish to practise resignation, unless it was quite necessary. I wanted to live deep and suck out all the marrow of life, to live so sturdily and Spartan-like as to put to rout all that was not life, to cut a broad swath and shave close, to drive life into a corner, and reduce it to its lowest terms, and, if it proved to be mean, why then to get the whole and genuine meanness of it, and publish its meanness to the world; or if it were sublime, to know it by experience, and be able to give a true account of it in my next excursion.

— Henry David Thoreau, Walden, "Where I Lived, and What I Lived For"[36]

Thoreau needed to concentrate and get himself working more on his writing. In March 1845, Ellery Channing told Thoreau, "Go out upon that, build yourself a hut, & there begin the grand process of devouring yourself alive. I see no other alternative, no other hope for you."[37] Two months later, Thoreau embarked on a two-year experiment in simple living on July 4, 1845, when he moved to a small, self-built house on land owned by Emerson in a second-growth forest around the shores of Walden Pond. The house was in "a pretty pasture and woodlot" of 14 acres (57,000 m2) that Emerson had bought,[38] 1.5 miles (2.4 km) from his family home.[39]

On July 24 or July 25, 1846, Thoreau ran into the local tax collector, Sam Staples, who asked him to pay six years of delinquent poll taxes. Thoreau refused because of his opposition to the Mexican-American War and slavery, and he spent a night in jail because of this refusal. The next day Thoreau was freed when someone, likely his aunt, paid the tax against his wishes.[40] The experience had a strong impact on Thoreau. In January and February 1848, he delivered lectures on "The Rights and Duties of the Individual in relation to Government"[41] explaining his tax resistance at the Concord Lyceum. Bronson Alcott attended the lecture, writing in his journal on January 26:

Heard Thoreau's lecture before the Lyceum on the relation of the individual to the State— an admirable statement of the rights of the individual to self-government, and an attentive audience. His allusions to the Mexican War, to Mr. Hoar's expulsion from Carolina, his own imprisonment in Concord Jail for refusal to pay his tax, Mr. Hoar's payment of mine when taken to prison for a similar refusal, were all pertinent, well considered, and reasoned. I took great pleasure in this deed of Thoreau's.

— Bronson Alcott, Journals (1938)[42]

Thoreau revised the lecture into an essay entitled Resistance to Civil Government (also known as Civil Disobedience). In May 1849 it was published by Elizabeth Peabody in the Aesthetic Papers. Thoreau had taken up a version of Percy Shelley's principle in the political poem The Mask of Anarchy (1819), that Shelley begins with the powerful images of the unjust forms of authority of his time—and then imagines the stirrings of a radically new form of social action.[43]

At Walden Pond, he completed a first draft of A Week on the Concord and Merrimack Rivers, an elegy to his brother, John, that described their 1839 trip to the White Mountains. Thoreau did not find a publisher for this book and instead printed 1,000 copies at his own expense, though fewer than 300 were sold.[31]:234 Thoreau self-published on the advice of Emerson, using Emerson's own publisher, Munroe, who did little to publicize the book.

In August 1846, Thoreau briefly left Walden to make a trip to Mount Katahdin in Maine, a journey later recorded in "Ktaadn", the first part of The Maine Woods.

Thoreau left Walden Pond on September 6, 1847.[31]:244 At Emerson's request, he immediately moved back into the Emerson house to help Lidian manage the household while her husband was on an extended trip to Europe.[44] Over several years, he worked to pay off his debts and also continuously revised his manuscript for what, in 1854, he would publish as Walden, or Life in the Woods, recounting the two years, two months, and two days he had spent at Walden Pond. The book compresses that time into a single calendar year, using the passage of four seasons to symbolize human development. Part memoir and part spiritual quest, Walden at first won few admirers, but later critics have regarded it as a classic American work that explores natural simplicity, harmony, and beauty as models for just social and cultural conditions.

American poet Robert Frost wrote of Thoreau, "In one book ... he surpasses everything we have had in America."[45]

American author John Updike said of the book: "A century and a half after its publication, Walden has become such a totem of the back-to-nature, preservationist, anti-business, civil-disobedience mindset, and Thoreau so vivid a protester, so perfect a crank and hermit saint, that the book risks being as revered and unread as the Bible."[46]

Thoreau moved out of Emerson's house in July 1848 and stayed at a home on Belknap Street nearby. In 1850, he and his family moved into a home at 255 Main Street; he stayed there until his death.[47]

Later years, 1851–1862

In 1851, Thoreau became increasingly fascinated with natural history and travel/expedition narratives. He read avidly on botany and often wrote observations on this topic into his journal. He admired William Bartram, and Charles Darwin's Voyage of the Beagle. He kept detailed observations on Concord's nature lore, recording everything from how the fruit ripened over time to the fluctuating depths of Walden Pond and the days certain birds migrated. The point of this task was to "anticipate" the seasons of nature, in his words.[48][49]

He became a land surveyor and continued to write increasingly detailed natural history observations about the 26 square miles (67 km2) town in his journal, a two-million word document he kept for 24 years. He also kept a series of notebooks, and these observations became the source for Thoreau's late natural history writings, such as Autumnal Tints, The Succession of Trees, and Wild Apples, an essay lamenting the destruction of indigenous and wild apple species.

Until the 1970s, literary critics[who?] dismissed Thoreau's late pursuits as amateur science and philosophy. With the rise of environmental history and ecocriticism, several new readings of this matter began to emerge, showing Thoreau to be both a philosopher and an analyst of ecological patterns in fields and woodlots.[50][51] For instance, his late essay, "The Succession of Forest Trees", shows that he used experimentation and analysis to explain how forests regenerate after fire or human destruction, through dispersal by seed-bearing winds or animals.

He traveled to Quebec once, Cape Cod four times, and Maine three times; these landscapes inspired his "excursion" books, A Yankee in Canada, Cape Cod, and The Maine Woods, in which travel itineraries frame his thoughts about geography, history and philosophy. Other travels took him southwest to Philadelphia and New York City in 1854, and west across the Great Lakes region in 1861, visiting Niagara Falls, Detroit, Chicago, Milwaukee, St. Paul and Mackinac Island.[52] Although provincial in his physical travels, he was extraordinarily well-read. He obsessively devoured all the first-hand travel accounts available in his day, at a time when the last unmapped regions of the earth were being explored. He read Magellan and James Cook, the arctic explorers Franklin, Mackenzie and Parry, David Livingstone and Richard Francis Burton on Africa, Lewis and Clark; and hundreds of lesser-known works by explorers and literate travelers.[53] Astonishing amounts of global reading fed his endless curiosity about the peoples, cultures, religions and natural history of the world, and left its traces as commentaries in his voluminous journals. He processed everything he read, in the local laboratory of his Concord experience. Among his famous aphorisms is his advice to "live at home like a traveler."[54]

After John Brown's raid on Harpers Ferry, many prominent voices in the abolitionist movement distanced themselves from Brown, or damned him with faint praise. Thoreau was disgusted by this, and he composed a speech—A Plea for Captain John Brown—which was uncompromising in its defense of Brown and his actions. Thoreau's speech proved persuasive: first the abolitionist movement began to accept Brown as a martyr, and by the time of the American Civil War entire armies of the North were literally singing Brown's praises. As a contemporary biographer of John Brown put it: "If, as Alfred Kazin suggests, without John Brown there would have been no Civil War, we would add that without the Concord Transcendentalists, John Brown would have had little cultural impact."[55]

Thoreau contracted tuberculosis in 1835 and suffered from it sporadically afterwards. In 1859, following a late-night excursion to count the rings of tree stumps during a rain storm, he became ill with bronchitis. His health declined over three years with brief periods of remission, until he eventually became bedridden. Recognizing the terminal nature of his disease, Thoreau spent his last years revising and editing his unpublished works, particularly The Maine Woods and Excursions, and petitioning publishers to print revised editions of A Week and Walden. He also wrote letters and journal entries until he became too weak to continue. His friends were alarmed at his diminished appearance and were fascinated by his tranquil acceptance of death. When his aunt Louisa asked him in his last weeks if he had made his peace with God, Thoreau responded: "I did not know we had ever quarreled."[56]

Aware he was dying, Thoreau's last words were "Now comes good sailing", followed by two lone words, "moose" and "Indian".[57] He died on May 6, 1862 at age 44. Bronson Alcott planned the service and read selections from Thoreau's works, and Channing presented a hymn.[58] Emerson wrote the eulogy spoken at his funeral.[59] Originally buried in the Dunbar family plot, he and members of his immediate family were eventually moved to Sleepy Hollow Cemetery (N42° 27' 53.7" W71° 20' 33") in Concord, Massachusetts.

Thoreau's friend Ellery Channing published his first biography, Thoreau the Poet-Naturalist, in 1873, and Channing and another friend Harrison Blake edited some poems, essays, and journal entries for posthumous publication in the 1890s. Thoreau's journals, which he often mined for his published works but which remained largely unpublished at his death, were first published in 1906 and helped to build his modern reputation. A new, expanded edition of the journals is underway, published by Princeton University Press. Today, Thoreau is regarded as one of the foremost American writers, both for the modern clarity of his prose style and the prescience of his views on nature and politics. His memory is honored by the international Thoreau Society and his legacy honored by the Thoreau Institute at Walden Woods, established in 1998 in Lincoln, Massachusetts.

Nature and human existence

Most of the luxuries and many of the so-called comforts of life are not only not indispensable, but positive hindrances to the elevation of mankind.

— Thoreau[60]

Thoreau was an early advocate of recreational hiking and canoeing, of conserving natural resources on private land, and of preserving wilderness as public land. He was not a strict vegetarian, though he said he preferred that diet[61] and advocated it as a means of self-improvement. He wrote in Walden: "The practical objection to animal food in my case was its uncleanness; and besides, when I had caught and cleaned and cooked and eaten my fish, they seemed not to have fed me essentially. It was insignificant and unnecessary, and cost more than it came to. A little bread or a few potatoes would have done as well, with less trouble and filth."[62]

Thoreau neither rejected civilization nor fully embraced wilderness. Instead he sought a middle ground, the pastoral realm that integrates both nature and culture. His philosophy required that he be a didactic arbitration between the wilderness he based so much on and the spreading mass of North American humanity. He decried the latter endlessly but felt the teachers need to be close to those who needed to hear what he wanted to tell them. The wildness he enjoyed was the nearby swamp or forest, and he preferred "partially cultivated country." His idea of being "far in the recesses of the wilderness" of Maine was to "travel the logger's path and the Indian trail", but he also hiked on pristine untouched land. In the essay "Henry David Thoreau, Philosopher" Roderick Nash writes: "Thoreau left Concord in 1846 for the first of three trips to northern Maine. His expectations were high because he hoped to find genuine, primeval America. But contact with real wilderness in Maine affected him far differently than had the idea of wilderness in Concord. Instead of coming out of the woods with a deepened appreciation of the wilds, Thoreau felt a greater respect for civilization and realized the necessity of balance."[63] On alcohol, Thoreau wrote: "I would fain keep sober always... I believe that water is the only drink for a wise man; wine is not so noble a liquor... Of all ebriosity, who does not prefer to be intoxicated by the air he breathes?"[62]

Politics

Thoreau was fervently against slavery and actively supported the abolitionist movement.[1] He participated in the Underground Railroad, delivered lectures that attacked the Fugitive Slave Law, and in opposition with the popular opinion of the time, supported radical abolitionist militia leader John Brown and his party.[1] Two weeks after the ill-fated raid on Harpers Ferry and in the weeks leading up to Brown's execution, Thoreau regularly delivered a speech to the citizens of Concord, Massachusetts in which he compared the American government to Pontius Pilate and likened Brown's execution to the crucifixion of Jesus Christ:

Some eighteen hundred years ago Christ was crucified; this morning, perchance, Captain Brown was hung. These are the two ends of a chain which is not without its links. He is not Old Brown any longer; he is an angel of light."[3]

In The Last Days of John Brown, Thoreau described the words and deeds of John Brown as noble and an example of heroism.[64] In addition, he lamented the newspaper editors who dismissed Brown and his scheme as "crazy".[64]

Thoreau was a proponent of limited government and individualism. Although he was hopeful that mankind could potentially have, through self-betterment, the kind of government which "governs not at all", he distanced himself from contemporary "no-government men" (anarchists), writing: "I ask for, not at once no government, but at once a better government."[5]

Thoreau deemed the evolution from absolute monarchy to limited monarchy to democracy as "a progress toward true respect for the individual" and theorized about further improvements "towards recognizing and organizing the rights of man."[5] Echoing this belief, he went on to write: "There will never be a really free and enlightened State until the State comes to recognize the individual as a higher and independent power, from which all its power and authority are derived, and treats him accordingly."[5]

Although Thoreau believed resistance to unjustly exercised authority could be both violent (exemplified in his support for John Brown) and nonviolent (his own example of tax resistance displayed in Resistance to Civil Government), he regarded pacifist nonresistance as temptation to passivity,[65] writing: "Let not our Peace be proclaimed by the rust on our swords, or our inability to draw them from their scabbards; but let her at least have so much work on her hands as to keep those swords bright and sharp."[65] Furthermore, in a formal lyceum debate in 1841, he debated the subject "Is it ever proper to offer forcible resistance?", arguing the affirmative.[66]

Likewise, his condemnation of the Mexican-American War did not stem from pacifism, but rather because he considered Mexico "unjustly overrun and conquered by a foreign army" as a means to expand the slave territory.[67]

Thoreau was ambivalent towards industrialization and capitalism. On one hand he regarded commerce as "unexpectedly confident and serene, adventurous, and unwearied"[3] and expressed admiration for its associated cosmopolitanism, writing:

I am refreshed and expanded when the freight train rattles past me, and I smell the stores which go dispensing their odors all the way from Long Wharf to Lake Champlain, reminding me of foreign parts, of coral reefs, and Indian oceans, and tropical climes, and the extent of the globe. I feel more like a citizen of the world at the sight of the palm-leaf which will cover so many flaxen New England heads the next summer.[3]

On the other hand, he wrote disparagingly of the factory system:

I cannot believe that our factory system is the best mode by which men may get clothing. The condition of the operatives is becoming every day more like that of the English; and it cannot be wondered at, since, as far as I have heard or observed, the principal object is, not that mankind may be well and honestly clad, but, unquestionably, that corporations may be enriched.[3]

Thoreau also favored bioregionalism, the protection of animals and wild areas, free trade, and taxation for schools and highways.[1] He disapproved of the subjugation of Native Americans, slavery, technological utopianism, consumerism, philistinism, mass entertainment, and frivolous applications of technology.[1]

Intellectual interests, influences, and affinities

Indian sacred texts and philosophy

Thoreau was influenced by Indian spiritual thought. In Walden, there are many overt references to the sacred texts of India. For example, in the first chapter ("Economy"), he writes: "How much more admirable the Bhagvat-Geeta than all the ruins of the East!"[3] American Philosophy: An Encyclopedia classes him as one of several figures who "took a more pantheist or pandeist approach by rejecting views of God as separate from the world",[68] also a characteristic of Hinduism.

Furthermore, in "The Pond in Winter", he equates Walden Pond with the sacred Ganges river, writing:

In the morning I bathe my intellect in the stupendous and cosmogonal philosophy of the Bhagvat Geeta since whose composition years of the gods have elapsed, and in comparison with which our modern world and its literature seem puny and trivial; and I doubt if that philosophy is not to be referred to a previous state of existence, so remote is its sublimity from our conceptions. I lay down the book and go to my well for water, and lo! there I meet the servant of the Brahmin, priest of Brahmaand Vishnu and Indra, who still sits in his temple on the Ganges reading the Vedas, or dwells at the root of a tree with his crust and water jug. I meet his servant come to draw water for his master, and our buckets as it were grate together in the same well. The pure Walden water is mingled with the sacred water of the Ganges.[3]

Additionally, Thoreau followed various Hindu customs, including following a diet of rice ("It was fit that I should live on rice, mainly, who loved so well the philosophy of India."[3]), flute playing (reminiscent of the favorite musical pastime of Krishna), and yoga.

In an 1849 letter to his friend H.G.O. Blake, he wrote about yoga and its meaning to him:

Free in this world as the birds in the air, disengaged from every kind of chains, those who practice yoga gather in Brahma the certain fruits of their works. Depend upon it that, rude and careless as I am, I would fain practice the yoga faithfully. The yogi, absorbed in contemplation, contributes in his degree to creation; he breathes a divine perfume, he hears wonderful things. Divine forms traverse him without tearing him, and united to the nature which is proper to him, he goes, he acts as animating original matter. To some extent, and at rare intervals, even I am a yogi.[69]

Biology

Thoreau read contemporary works in the new science of biology, including the works of Alexander von Humboldt, Charles Darwin, and Asa Gray (Charles Darwin's staunchest American ally).[70]

In 1859, Thoreau purchased and read Darwin's On the Origin of Species.

Unlike many natural historians at the time, including Louis Agassiz who publicly opposed Darwinism in favor of a static view of nature, Thoreau was immediately enthusiastic about the theory of evolution by natural selection and endorsed it,[71] stating:

The development theory implies a greater vital force in Nature, because it is more flexible and accommodating, and equivalent to a sort of constant new creation. (A quote from On the Origin of Species follows this sentence.)[70]

Influence

"Thoreau's careful observations and devastating conclusions have rippled into time, becoming stronger as the weaknesses Thoreau noted have become more pronounced ... Events that seem to be completely unrelated to his stay at Walden Pond have been influenced by it, including the national park system, the British labor movement, the creation of India, the civil rights movement, the hippie revolution, the environmental movement, and the wilderness movement. Today, Thoreau's words are quoted with feeling by liberals, socialists, anarchists, libertarians, and conservatives alike."

— Ken Kifer[72]

Thoreau's political writings had little impact during his lifetime, as "his contemporaries did not see him as a theorist or as a radical, viewing him instead as a naturalist. They either dismissed or ignored his political essays, including Civil Disobedience. The only two complete books (as opposed to essays) published in his lifetime, Walden and A Week on the Concord and Merrimack Rivers (1849), both dealt with nature, in which he loved to wander."[15] His obituary was lumped in with others rather than as a separate article in an 1862 yearbook.[73] Nevertheless, Thoreau's writings went on to influence many public figures. Political leaders and reformers like Mohandas Gandhi, U.S. President John F. Kennedy, American civil rights activist Martin Luther King, Jr., U.S. Supreme Court Justice William O. Douglas, and Russian author Leo Tolstoy all spoke of being strongly affected by

Thoreau's work, particularly Civil Disobedience, as did "right-wing theorist Frank Chodorov [who] devoted an entire issue of his monthly, Analysis, to an appreciation of Thoreau."[74]

Thoreau also influenced many artists and authors including Edward Abbey, Willa Cather, Marcel Proust, William Butler Yeats, Sinclair Lewis, Ernest Hemingway, Upton Sinclair,[75] E. B. White, Lewis Mumford,[76] Frank Lloyd Wright, Alexander Posey[77] and Gustav Stickley.[78] Thoreau also influenced naturalists like John Burroughs, John Muir, E. O. Wilson, Edwin Way Teale, Joseph Wood Krutch, B. F. Skinner, David Brower and Loren Eiseley, whom Publishers Weekly called "the modern Thoreau."[79] English writer Henry Stephens Salt wrote a biography of Thoreau in 1890, which popularized Thoreau's ideas in Britain: George Bernard Shaw, Edward Carpenter and Robert Blatchford were among those who became Thoreau enthusiasts as a result of Salt's advocacy.[80] Mohandas Gandhi first read Walden in 1906 while working as a civil rights activist in Johannesburg, South Africa. He first read Civil Disobedience "while he sat in a South African prison for the crime of nonviolently protesting discrimination against the Indian population in the Transvaal. The essay galvanized Gandhi, who wrote and published a synopsis of Thoreau's argument, calling its 'incisive logic ... unanswerable' and referring to Thoreau as 'one of the greatest and most moral men America has produced'."[81][82] He told American reporter Webb Miller, "[Thoreau's] ideas influenced me greatly. I adopted some of them and recommended the study of Thoreau to all of my friends who were helping me in the cause of Indian Independence. Why I actually took the name of my movement from Thoreau's essay 'On the Duty of Civil Disobedience,' written about 80 years ago."[83]

Martin Luther King, Jr. noted in his autobiography that his first encounter with the idea of non-violent resistance was reading "On Civil Disobedience" in 1944 while attending Morehouse College. He wrote in his autobiography that it was, "Here, in this courageous New Englander's refusal to pay his taxes and his choice of jail rather than support a war that would spread slavery's territory into Mexico, I made my first contact with the theory of nonviolent resistance. Fascinated by the idea of refusing to cooperate with an evil system, I was so deeply moved that I reread the work several times. I became convinced that noncooperation with evil is as much a moral obligation as is cooperation with good. No other person has been more eloquent and passionate in getting this idea across than Henry David Thoreau. As a result of his writings and personal witness, we are the heirs of a legacy of creative protest. The teachings of Thoreau came alive in our civil rights movement; indeed, they are more alive than ever before. Whether expressed in a sit-in at lunch counters, a freedom ride into Mississippi, a peaceful protest in Albany, Georgia, a bus boycott in Montgomery, Alabama, these are outgrowths of Thoreau's insistence that evil must be resisted and that no moral man can patiently adjust to injustice."[84]

American psychologist B. F. Skinner wrote that he carried a copy of Thoreau's Walden with him in his youth.[85] and, in 1945, wrote Walden Two, a fictional utopia about 1,000 members of a community living together inspired by the life of Thoreau.[86] Thoreau and his fellow Transcendentalists from Concord were a major inspiration of the composer Charles Ives. The 4th movement of the Concord Sonata for piano (with a part for flute, Thoreau's instrument) is a character picture and he also set Thoreau's words.[87]

In the early 1960s Allen Sherman referred to Thoreau in his song parody "Here's To Crabgrass" about the suburban housing boom of that era with the line "Come let us go there and live like Thoreau there."

Actor Ron Thompson did a dramatic portrayal of Henry David Thoreau on the 1976 NBC television series The Rebels.[88][89]

Thoreau's ideas have impacted and resonated with various strains in the anarchist movement, with Emma Goldman referring to him as "the greatest American anarchist."[90] Green anarchism and Anarcho-primitivism in particular have both derived inspiration and ecological points-of-view from the writings of Thoreau. John Zerzan included Thoreau's text "Excursions" (1863) in his edited compilation of works in the anarcho-primitivist tradition titled Against civilization: Readings and reflections.[91] Additionally, Murray Rothbard, the founder of anarcho-capitalism, has opined that Thoreau was one of the "great intellectual heroes" of his movement.[74] Thoreau was also an important influence on late-19th-century anarchist naturism.[92][93] Globally, Thoreau's concepts also held importance within individualist anarchist circles[94][95] in Spain,[92][93][94] France,[94][96] and Portugal.[97]

Criticism

Although his writings would receive widespread acclaim, Thoreau's ideas were not universally applauded. Scottish author Robert Louis Stevenson judged Thoreau's endorsement of living alone and apart from modern society in natural simplicity to be a mark of "unmanly" effeminacy and "womanish solitude", while deeming him a self-indulgent "skulker."[98] Nathaniel Hawthorne was also critical of Thoreau, writing that he "repudiated all regular modes of getting a living, and seems inclined to lead a sort of Indian life among civilized men."[99][100] In a similar vein, poet John Greenleaf Whittier detested what he deemed to be the "wicked" and "heathenish" message of Walden, claiming that Thoreau wanted man to "lower himself to the level of a woodchuck and walk on four legs."[101]

In response to such criticisms, English novelist George Eliot, writing for the Westminster Review, characterized such critics as uninspired and narrow-minded:

People—very wise in their own eyes—who would have every man's life ordered according to a particular pattern, and who are intolerant of every existence the utility of which is not palpable to them, may pooh-pooh Mr. Thoreau and this episode in his history, as unpractical and dreamy.[102]

Thoreau himself also responded to the criticism in a paragraph of his work "Walden" (1854), by illustrating the irrelevance of their inquiries:

I should not obtrude my affairs so much on the notice of my readers if very particular inquiries had not been made by my townsmen concerning my mode of life, which some would call impertinent, though they do not appear to me at all impertinent, but, considering the circumstances, very natural and pertinent. Some have asked what I got to eat; if I did not feel lonesome; if I was not afraid; and the like. Others have been curious to learn what portion of my income I devoted to charitable purposes; and some, who have large families, how many poor children I maintained. [...] Unfortunately, I am confined to this theme by the narrowness of my experience. Moreover, I, on my side, require of every writer, first or last, a simple and sincere account of his own life, and not merely what he has heard of other men's lives; [...] I trust that none will stretch the seams in putting on the coat, for it may do good service to him whom it fits.[103]

Recent criticism has accused Thoreau of hypocrisy, misanthropy and being sanctimonious, based on his writings in Walden,[104] although this criticism has been perceived as highly selective.[105][106][107]

Printed in Great Britain
by Amazon